of course
I LOVE YOU
Thoughts on Marriage

OF COURSE

I

LOVE

YOU

Albert J. Nimeth O.F.M.

INTRODUCTION

MARRIAGE is an act of faith in which one person puts the meaning and happiness of his life into the hands of another. It is a gift of oneself. The acceptance of the gift depends on the other. Even when the gift is accepted, there is no guarantee that things will turn out well or that love will endure. But if each person works honestly and sincerely to be the best person he can be, there is reason to believe the union will succeed. Durability will depend on how successfully the couple can harmonize all the aspects of their life together. Basically marriage is a human relationship. Given good will, there is hope that if one fails, he will not fail forever; if one is hurt, he will heal. This calls for faith in oneself and faith in the other.

—Albert J. Nimeth O.F.M.

Once you have chosen your partner, let it remain forever. Then devote your time to preparing it for domestic use. Some keep a partner in a pickle; others, in hot water. Even the poorest variety can be made sweet and tender and good by a garnish of patience. Sweeten well with smiles and flavor with kisses. Wrap in a mantle of charity, keep warm with a steady fire of understanding. Serve often with peaches and cream. Thus prepared your partner will last for years.

— Adapted

MARRIAGE IS
  an interesting adventure
  a hazardous risk.
Human love alone
  will not
  guarantee success.
Marriage needs
  GOD
  to bolster and uplift
  LOVE.
Divine help
  broadens and deepens
  human love
    transforming it
    stabilizing it.
Whatever is clouded
  becomes clear.
Whatever is harsh
  becomes gentle
    if
    GOD IS THERE.

The SACRAMENT of matrimony
  (for the believer)
  is like a credit card
  to be used
  for God's help
  when stress and strain
     take their toll;
     when the path of love
     gets rough.
GOD is not to be
  the last resort.
He is the FIRST.
Marriage is a sign
  and source
  of special graces
  which perfect
     NATURAL LOVE
     and cement
     the bond of unity.

*And look into space; you shall see Him
walking in the cloud, outstretching
His arms in the lightning and descending
rain. You shall see Him smiling in
flowers, then rising and waving His
hands in trees.*

— *Kahil Gibran*

This unity is created
　by MUTUAL love and support.
MUTUAL is important for
　marriage is never
　　a one-way street.

MORE and more
　marriage is looked upon
　as a COVENANT,
　less as a CONTRACT.
A covenant is
　expansive, all-embracing.
A contract is
　restrictive, limiting.

P. F. Palmer writes:
　"Contracts deal with things,
　　covenants with people.
Contracts are best understood
　by lawyers,
　　covenants are appreciated
　　by poets.

Contracts are made by children
who know the value of a penny
covenants can be made
only by adults who are
mentally
emotionally
spiritually
MATURE."

*Maturity is an ability to deal with
reality constructively.*

*Maturity is a capacity to change
gracefully*

*Maturity is finding satisfaction in giving
rather than receiving.*

*Maturity is ability to relate to others
consistently in a mutually satisfying
manner.*

*Maturity is the capacity to direct hostile
energy into constructive outlets.*

LOVE is of the essence.
Lovers want
  the good of the other
  and show it
    by thoughtfulness
    and physical gestures
    from embraces to kisses
    to complete sexual union.

All the forces
  of body and soul
  are marshalled
  to show love.

Most people have
  a greater capacity for love
  than they ever put to use.

*Our ability to love depends on our ability
to find ways and means of expressing it.
For this we need faith in ourselves.*

Love does not ask
  What MUST I do?
  What is my OBLIGATION?
This is not the language
  of love.
This begins to set limits.
As soon as we set limits,
  love begins to erode.
Like the wedding ring
  it has NO END.

Love never sets limits.
Love asks,
  WHAT MORE CAN I DO?
"Greater love no one has
    than this — that he
    be willing
    to lay down his life."

SEX, of course,
 is important.
Love, however, can endure
 without sex,
 but sex without love
  goes stale.
To be a proof of love
 the gratification of sex
 must enhance
 the deep personal
 and spiritual content
 of the union.
Without this
 people become objects
 and sex a mere exchange of service
 rather than a rich
  personal SHARING.

It is not sufficient to love mechanically, perfunctorily and mutely. You have to dramatize it from time to time.

If the only connection
  is physical
  the union is unstable
  for man is
      MORE THAN BODY.
Even in the use of sex
   the way to LIFE
        human
        spiritual
        divine
   must be kept open.

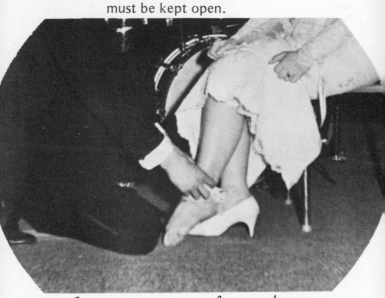

Learn to communicate by a word, a touch, a gesture, a glance in a way that they are easily understood.

A good LOVE-MAKER
does not necessarily
make a good LOVER.
A perfect duet
takes time and practice.
A blustering know-it-all male
who rushes his wife
to the portal of love-making
and drags her through
without regard for sensibility
is juvenile and selfish.
Should she hesitate or demur
she needs guidance
and encouragement
not petulance
not resentment.
It is juvenile and selfish
to care more about
PERSONAL pleasure
than MUTUAL pleasure.
It is unfair
to grasp avidly
for pleasure and passion
without deep understanding
without genuine concern
without real love.

Candid discussions
  about what pleases
  and displeases
  in sexual embrace
    are important and necessary.
There is always
  something to learn
    some revelation to make
    some excitement to display
      some enjoyment to enhance.
The goal is
  to further love
  and mutual joy.
To withhold, in this matter,
  care and concern
  bespeaks
    insensitivity
    indolence
      brutishness.

Each partner must feel free to discover his or her unique way of expressing wishes, desires and needs as they occur, spontaneously and naturally, never by the numbers according to a book.

— *Johnson/Masters*

Love is not only
  a matter of PASSION.
It is also
  a matter of COMPASSION.

Loving and love-making
  are two streams
  that must
      BLEND COMPLETELY.

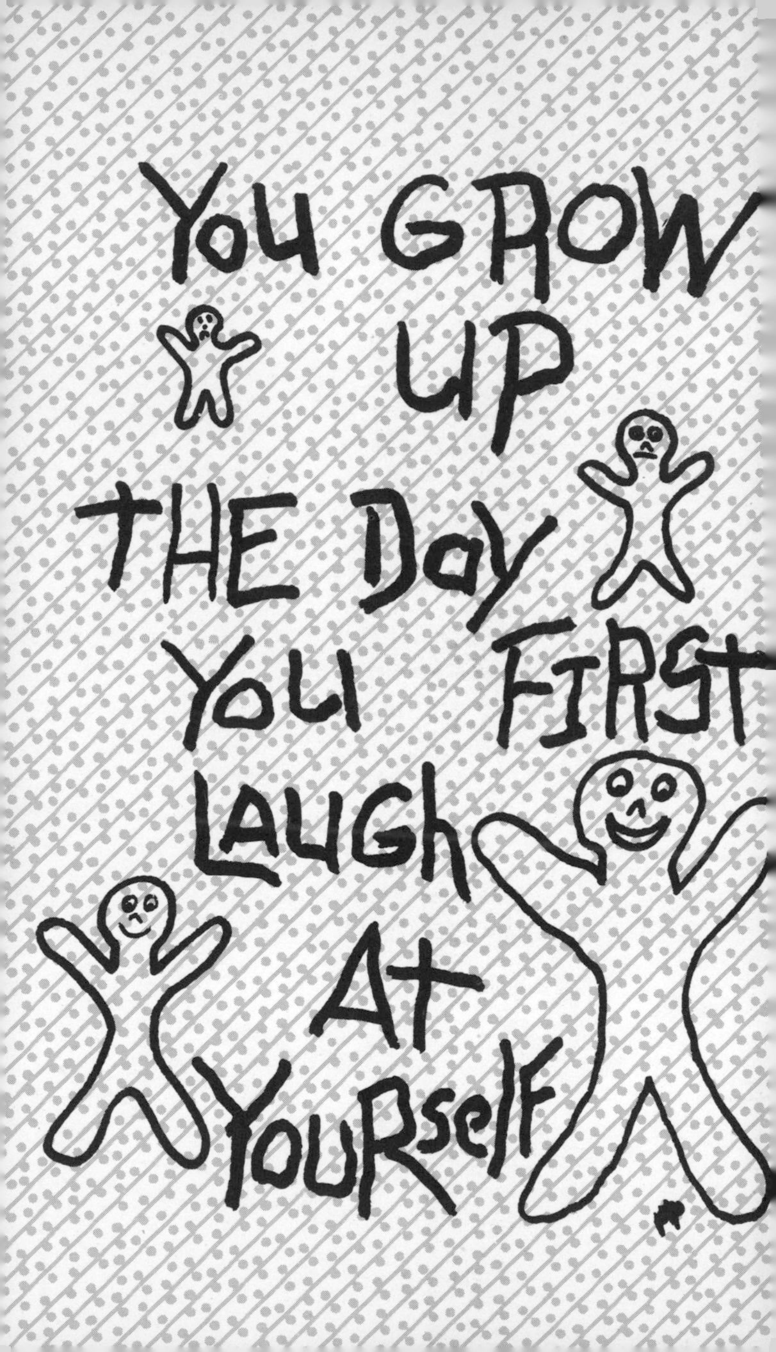
YOU GROW UP
THE DAY
YOU FIRST
LAUGH
AT
YOURSELF

George J. Nathan:
"The man and woman
  who can laugh
  at their love,
  who can kiss
  with smiles,
embrace with chuckles,
  will outlast
IN MUTUAL AFFECTION
  all throat-lumpy
  cow-eyed couples.
Nothing lives on
  so fresh and ever green
  as the love
    WITH A FUNNYBONE."

Humor is an affirmation of dignity, a declaration of man's superiority to all that befalls him.

— *Romain Gary*

GENUINE LOVE is needed
to endure the shock
of discovery
that much of wife's beauty
comes from the drugstore,
or husband has a passion
for a golf course.

It takes genuine love
to survive
the rantings and ravings
the quirks and follies
the clay feet.

It takes genuine love
to remain loyal
despite everyday frictions
and occasional outbursts.

FIDELITY is paramount.
Marriage creates
  an inner circle
  that is EXCLUSIVE —
  ONE man, ONE woman.
To be footloose
  free and fancy
  as if unattached
  within this circle
  is CONTRABAND.

This does not mean
  you can't look.
Even if you are
  on a diet
  you can admire
  the menu.

"Breathes there a man
  with soul so dead
  who never stopped
  and turned his head
  and said
  "not bad."

Nevertheless,
  open marriage
  despite popularity
  CREATES more problems
  than it SOLVES.
We can kid ourselves
  just so far
  before the kickback comes
  relentless and violent.
Fidelity is
  SAFE and SANE.
Fidelity is also
  RIGHT.

Let there be spaces in your togetherness,
And let the winds of heaven dance
  between you.
Fill each other's cup but drink not
  from one cup.
Give one another of your bread but eat
  not from the same loaf.
Sing and dance together and be joyous
But let each one of you be alone,
Even as the strings of a lute are alone
  though they quiver with the same music.
                              — Kahil Gibran

Happiness in marriage
  essentially means
  HUMAN ADJUSTMENT.

This adjustment
  has to take place
  in an intimacy
  from which only death
  provides an escape.

Adjustment is ever
  an on-going process
  of coping satisfactorily
    with demands
    with strains
      with frustrations
      with conflicts
        with confrontations.

Adjustment calls for
 MATURITY
 which accepts
   self-discipline
   self-sacrifice.

Mature people
 do not have to be
 compelled to do
 what has to be done.
They do it
 without making it
 a federal case.

Mature adjustment
  accepts the fact
  that for every advantage of marriage
  a corresponding liberty
  is affected.
Marriage gives strength
  but demands
  ACCOUNTABILITY.
Marriage gives social stability
  but curtails
  social activity.
Marriage gives solace
  but demands
  SURRENDER.

For this one needs
  resiliency
      the ability to bounce back
      the ability to keep changing
      because LIFE itself
      is a constant, relentless,
      mystifying change.

Adjustment is
 always dynamic
 never static.
It does not mean
 giving up
 INDIVIDUALITY.
This individuality is necessary
 for the RICHNESS of life together.
This richness comes
 only if each maintains
 his uniqueness,
 develops it,
 and encourages partner
 to develop.
Not to do so
 impoverishes the union.
Two people
 shaped by their own experiences,
 put into a context
 where each can draw
 the best from the other,
 will grow if they seek
   the newness
     the excitement
     the surprise
       deep inside.
Not to grow
 is not to live.

It is sheer folly
  to imagine that
  man and woman
  have identical attitudes.
It is not a matter
  of higher or lower rungs
  on the same ladder.
It is a matter of
  different ladders.

An orchestra sounds rich and beautiful because each player is true to his role.

This difference,
  deeper than physical and educational,
  exasperates
      and attracts.
It cannot be ignored.

A man who claims he can read his wife like a book is illiterate.

To interpret behaviour of partner
in terms of one's own makeup
and particular psychology
leads to
    confusion
      misunderstanding
      misjudgement
        insecurity.

Marriage is not
 a perpetual petting party.
During courtship
 lovers tend
    to imagine similarities
     to ignore defects
       to minimize differences.

Strange how obvious
 faults become AFTER marriage.
The true picture
 comes into focus
 when the dashing hero
 growls when hungry,
 explodes purple when crossed.
Reality will out
 when the darling of courtship
 reveals she has
    a temper
     nerves
       odd ways.

These moments of enlightenment,
 if accepted
 with courage and wisdom,
 will spare many future regrets.

In the intimacy of marriage,
  despite good will,
  pain is inflicted
  without realizing it.
If something is not right,
  admit it.
Sometimes one must
  LET OUT FEELINGS.
Crises do not
  destroy love.
To imagine everything is fine
  when it isn't,
  is playing ostrich.
To grin and bear it
  is to play the cynic.
To blame your partner rashly
  is to play the fool.
To blame some unchangeable trait
  of your own
  is the play of the fatalist.

Find out
 WHAT IS!
Marriage can thrive
 only on REALITY.
If something goes wrong
 it is futile
 to fence with
  A WINDMILL.

SELF-CONTROL in marriage
  is imperative.
Without it
  havoc ensues.

One has to say
  NO
  to some feelings and emotions.
One has to REFINE
  some feelings and emotions.

More important
  one has to learn
  to CHANNEL
  feelings and emotions
  toward a USEFUL PURPOSE.

Instead of taking it out
  on your partner,
  use the same energy
  to BUILD
  the relationship.

If you must object,
   object to the person involved
   not to others.
Object in private.
Object to what can be changed.
Object to one thing at a time.

If the disagreements are
   major
      frequent
         long-standing
            seek outside help.

*If you must find fault, imitate the barber
who lathers the face to soften the pull
of the razor.*

OF COURSE, it is all right
　for each to have
　special friends.
You simply cannot be
　EVERYTHING
　to each other.
There are needs
　that other companions and friends
　can fulfill.

It is wise, however,
　to have as many
　mutual friends as possible.

Here's a yardstick:
How do they get along
　as husband and wife?
What are their main interests?
What is their attitude
　　Toward marriage?
　　　Toward spending time?
　　　Toward happiness?
　　　Toward God?

Besides mutual friends
  MUTUAL INTERESTS
  are important and necessary.
These must be
  developed and cultivated.
There must be
  areas of MUTUAL INTEREST
  that are exclusive —
  your own little world
  reserved for yourselves only.
Where children are involved
  they are not to be used
  as a buffer
  to keep partners apart.
This defeats the goal of developing
  an exclusive common ground
  of enduring enjoyable interest.
This is a never-ending process
  to the very end.
Only then can one be assured that
  when everyone else is gone
    when many dreams have vanished
      when the fires become embers
        when there is just the two of you
  you will find each other
    interesting
    lovable
      enjoyable.

There is no reason
why he can't
go on his fishing trip.
There is no reason
why she can't
have her bridge club.
Going apart
is not bad
GROWING apart
is very bad.

Love does not consist in gazing at each other but in looking together in the same direction.

— Antoine De Saint-Expuery

Taking each other
　for granted
　is bad.

Portia complains:
"Within the bond of marriage, tell me Brutus,
　Is it expected that I should know no secret
　That appertains to you? Am I yourself,
　But as it were, in sort of limitation,
　To keep with you at meals, comfort your bed
　And talk with you sometimes
　Dwell within the suburbs
　Of your good pleasure. If I be no more
　Portia is Brutus' harlot, not his wife."

It is hard for a wife
  to accept that a man's
  desire to achieve
  is not linked exclusively
  with his family and home.
Sometimes a man
  has to achieve,
  just to achieve.
At times a wife
  can be in competition
    with his job
    with his profession
    with his hobby.
The difficulty is compounded
  because his day seems studded
    with accomplishments
    with challenge
    with diversion
    with risk
    with pleasure.
Her day, by contrast, seems
  routine
  dull
    monotonous.

*Remember always that you have not
only the right to be an individual; you
have an obligation to be one.*
                    — *Eleanor Roosevelt*

All the more reason
  why he must share
  the enriching aspects
  of his life.
He can enrich her life
  with the spice of variety
  with the flavor of the struggle.

More than merely receiving,
  a wife, on her own,
  must continue to grow
  AS A PERSON.

Being a wife
  and being a mother
  are really temporary roles.
Being a PERSON is permanent.
To concentrate all resources
  into filling a temporary role
  to the neglect of the permanent
  is short-sighted.

Listen to your mother-in-law. Listen very carefully to her advice. But you don't have to follow it.

It is paramount
  that a wife have
  interests of her own.
She must seek
  new outlets
  new vistas.
She has to reach out,
  stretching
      her talents
        her abilities
          her opportunities.
The difference between
  being in a rut
  and in a grave
  is a matter of depth.
And when a person stops growing
  he is dead.

A VERY UNCOMFORTABLE
  place to live
  is beyond one's means.
In accumulation and use
  of material goods
  good management
  prudent spending
  self-control
      help distinguish between
      what we NEED and
      what we WANT.
Our needs are few
  and easily satisfied.
Our wants are many
  and seldom satisfied.
To stay within limits
  one must strive
      TO REGULATE NEEDS
      TO LIMIT WANTS.

If material goods
  work a strain on the marriage,
  PRIORITIES
      must be reassessed.

A very uncomfortable place to live is beyond your means.

Possessions are to be used
　　with enthusiasm
　　with gratitude
　　with caution.
They are a means to an end
　　not an end in themselves.
Creatures somehow
　　must lead to the
　　　CREATOR.

*A baby is God's opinion that the world
should go on.*

— Carl Sandburg

WHEN a man discovers
his wife is a doll
with reactions of a child
in the body of a woman,
    the reality can shock.
When a woman discovers
her husband is a stuffed-shirt
who panics when his temperature is up
who won't play if he can't win,
    the disillusion runs deep.
This is infantilism —
physically mature
but still a child
    intellectually
    emotionally.
Unless one can hasten
the growing-up process
the union is
    in jeopardy.
It is infantile
to get one's way
    by screaming
    by pouting
        by a tantrum
        by blackmailing with
            "if you don't do it,
            you don't love me."

It is obtuse to imagine
   all a woman needs are
      clothes on her back
      food on her table
      roof over her head.

She needs these
   but she also needs
      AFFECTION.

Many marriages go sour
   more from
      emotional starvation
      than sexual inadequacy.

Love must be given
   tangible form
   on emotional level.
It must be made
   to sparkle again and again
   by spontaneous affirmation
   generously rendered.

True love will sense
   the time and place
   when signs are needed

A considerate husband
  is always aware
  his wife is a
  living
  throbbing
  physical
  human being who needs to be
      respected
        fondled
          caressed.
She needs
  emotional love
  emotional support.
She needs to be
  TOLD she is loved.

She looks for signs of affection
  from her husband
    in his eyes
      in his voice
        in his attitude
          in his body language.
A woman wants to know
  that she pleasures her husband
  on all levels.
Her love for him
  is the heartbeat of her life
  and she must hear
    his emotional echo.

If love is unspoken
  because it is self-evident
  something rich and beautiful
    is DENIED.
These signs of affection
  must travel also
  from WIFE to HUSBAND.
Given this kind
  of care and attention,
  the opening buds
  of loving and love-making
  will blossom into
  a flower of
    beautiful full mutual satisfaction.

THAT WOMAN is self-defeating
   who, once she has her man,
   throws away the calorie counter,
   disregards her appearance,
   becomes sloven,
      fat and untidy.

Even at home, a wife
   should doll up.
Hours of practice during courtship
   can keep this routine
   to a minimum.

A husband needs to know
   that a wife cares
   by the way
   she cares for herself.

A husband who neglects
      his physical appearance
      his manners
      his diction
      his cleanliness
         is grossly uncouth.

It is not the big things
   that erode a union.
You can sit on a mountain
   but you cannot sit on a tack.

The little annoyances
      a vulgar belch
         boisterous bias
            body odor
               hackneyed cliches
                  no sense of humor
                     militate against
                        a happy marriage.

Even a tiny pebble
   in your shoe
   is unbearable.

*Many a marital grave is dug by a series
of little digs.*

A MAN CONVINCED AGAINST HIS WILL IS OF THE SAME OPINION STILL

STOP COMPLAINING.
It is futile.
It's like trying
  to beat down a wall
  with your head.
The wall stands.
You get a headache.
Why not look for
  A GATE?
Try a tender approach.

Recall fable of wind and sun.
Each tried to make
  the traveler shed his coat.
The wind huffed and puffed.
To no avail.
The more he huffed and puffed
  the tighter the man clung
  to his coat.
The sun shone
  GENTLY, KINDLY, WARMLY.
The traveler
  shed his coat.

A bad temper
　is just that —
　　BAD.

Right premise:
"You know I have a bad temper."
Wrong conclusion:
"Why don't you leave me alone?"
Right conclusion:
"I should do something about it
　　NOW."

Hotheads make life
　HOT.
If the mere mention
　of a subject,
　festers a wound,
　　why bring it up?
Why kick against the goad?

Some confrontations
　are good and necessary.
Some confrontations
　are unproductive and futile.
Gauge importance of the subject
　twenty-five years from now.
What difference
　will it make THEN?

STOP breathing
  down each other's neck.
Stop backing each other
  into a corner.
Be patient.

Expect mistakes
  but recognize them
      AS MISTAKES
      not as proper conduct.

Hang loose.
We all need freedom to relax.
Don't force your partner
  to weigh everything said and done.

This above all; to thine own self be true,
And it must follow, as night the day
Thou canst not then be false to any man.
                        — Shakespeare

Even in the face of hardship
  one must be TRUE TO HIMSELF
  even if it means
      A FIRM "NO."
This may be
  what your partner
      NEEDS
      and deep down WANTS.

Not every aggravation
  can be avoided.
Quarrel, if you must,
  but make the reconciliation
    SPEEDY and COMPLETE.
Never go to bed
    MAD.
If need be
  keep the lights burning
    ALL NIGHT.

Be aware that quarrels
  are tricky.
Often they have
  nothing to do
  with subject under fire.

Quarrels often are cover-ups
  for frustrations
  for boredom
  for deficiencies
      for insecurity
  for reluctance to face facts
  for forcing one's will
  for stupidity.
Look beneath the surface.
  It takes a lot of effort
      to see needs of others
      to anticipate wishes
      to adjust plans
        to give unsolicited affection.

Harmony is not automatic.
In marriage there are
  two unique individuals
  distinctly free
  with particular patterns
    of feeling and behaviour
      of background and desires
        of motives and intelligence
        of whims and impulses.

Daily intimate contact
  is bound to produce friction
  unless lubricated
    with consideration
    with tolerance
      with understanding
      with sympathy.

*We cannot learn from one another until
we stop shouting at one another —
until we speak quietly enough so that
our words can be heard as well as our
voices.*

— Richard Nixon

It helps to work out
  A SET OF SIGNALS.
If HE had a hard day at work,
  had a flat tire,
  heard the boss bark at him,
    why not WEAR HAT
          AT A TILT.

If SHE blew a fuse,
  burned a pot roast,
  was irritated by the children,
    why not TURN APRON
          BACKWARDS.

When the flares are out,
  caution is the rule.
Tread softly because
  atmosphere is charged
  dynamite is stored
    the wick is short.
Look for these signals,
  the obvious and the subtle.

RESPECT THEM to avoid
  stepping on toes
    provoking petty squabbles
    disrupting harmony.

It is dreadful and cheap
  to RIDICULE each other
  in public or private
    by sarcasm
      by deliberate digs
      by nit-picking
        by bruising an open sore.
Marriage does not absolve
  from courtesy
    from decency
      from respect.
During courtship one strives
  to create a good impression
    to develop an even disposition
    to please.
Finish the task.
Strive earnestly for
  cheerfulness
  helpfulness
  tact
    thoughtfulness
      meekness
      politeness
      kindness
        gentleness
          graciousness
          generosity
          loyalty.

When was the last time you wrote a love-letter?

Why do LOVE-LETTERS
   stop at the altar?
Love doesn't!
Why not write
   an occasional love-letter
   to be read at leisure
   unobserved.
It is the unexpected discovery
   that thrills.

The joy of loving is the joy of giving.

GIVE HAPPINESS!
One good way
  to give happiness
  is by accepting gifts
  GRACIOUSLY.
If we know
  how to accept a gift
  with GOOD GRACE,
  we increase partner's
  JOY OF GIVING.
So what if —
  color is wrong
  size too large
  price not right?
You can exchange it
  IN SECRET.
For the time being
  accept it
  in the SPIRIT GIVEN.
Enhance the pleasure
  of the GIVER.

If you are always on time
  and your partner always late,
    turn your clocks ahead.
If you are always late
  and your partner always on time,
    turn yourself ahead.

FEELING SORRY for oneself
  can hinder
  happiness in marriage.
It leads to exaggeration.
Self-pity inflates a problem·
  out of proportion.
Self-pity stimulates
  the imagination
  which quickly distorts.
A rule of thumb:
  "Don't feel more
  sorry for yourself
  than others
  feel for you."

Walk on the sunny side.
There is no merit
  in a long, sad face
  even if a pious person
  is wearing one.
Train yourself to see
  THE BRIGHT SIDE.
It takes discipline.
Nothing crushes effectively
  a healthy married spirit
  as quickly as
      glumness
        moroseness
          sulkiness
            pettiness.
Look for redeeming features.
Like the oyster
  create a PEARL
  from a bit of irritation.

Learn to LAUGH
  at yourself.
Learn to LAUGH
  WITH your partner.
See the HUMOR
  in life.
Humor is the ability
  to turn from
  the serious and tragic
  and SMILE.
It is the ability
  to RELAX.
Mild, gentle humor
  quickly relieves
    tensions
      conflicts
        stresses.
He who laughs —
  LASTS.

*You grow up the day you first laugh
at yourself.*
                    — Ethel Barrymore

WORRY destroys
  happiness in marriage.
Worry is
  AN ACQUIRED HABIT.
So it can be
  "Unacquired."
Worry puts one
  on a TREADMILL.
One keeps asking
  the SAME questions
  over and over again
  and not sitting still
  long enough
  to get an answer.
Most of the things
  one worries about
  NEVER happen.
Just when we need
  our energy
  to solve a problem
  it is dissipated
  in an exercise
  OF FUTILITY.

Happiness in marriage
  should not depend on
  a circumstance
  beyond your control.
If you can
  change the situation,
  CHANGE IT.
If you cannot
  change the situation,
  change YOUR ATTITUDE
  toward the situation.

Ask yourself:
  Is this MY problem?
If not, why sweat it?
Do I have to solve it
  NOW?
If not, wait.
If urgent
  what can I REALLY do?
Here two extremes
  are taboo —
  exaggerating the problem
  minimizing one's ability.
If objective scrutiny
  reveals, NOTHING
  can be done,
  I live with it.
If something
  can be done,
  I do it.
Worry neither
  solves a problem
  nor helps to live
  with it.

Oh Lord, give me the Serenity to
accept the things I cannot change; the
Courage to change the things that I can
and the Good Sense to know the
difference.

Keep a neat house,
 but don't be
 A FUSS BERTHA.
A home is for
 living and
 relaxing.
A SENSIBLE husband
 prefers a good-natured wife
 to an immaculately spotless home.

*Many a man has turned into a mule
because his wife was a nag.*

Besides, there is no reason
 why HE should not
 do his share
 to keep the home tidy.
If you show your wifely affection
 by picking up after him
  his socks
   his pipe
    his paper
     his rubbish,
      remember: "If you bend down
      the day you're wed,
      you'll bend down
      until you're dead."

You can live
  in the same house;
  put your feet
  under the same table;
  sleep between the same sheets
  and still be isolated and
    poles apart.
Union of body
  is not enough.
There has to be
  union of mind and soul.
Once married
  EVERYTHING must be viewed within,
  NOTHING divorced from,
    context of intimate relationship.
Mutual happiness
  is commensurate with
  ability to accept completely
    this RELATEDNESS.

JEALOUSY is egotistic,
 selfish and sly.
It grossly distorts.
It undermines
 trust of self
 trust of partner.
Partners are NOT PROPERTIES
 to be treated as one pleases
 as long as treatment
  is private.
Partners are PEOPLE
 with equal rights.
When either party
 monopolizes the other,
 demanding constant,
 ceaseless attention,
  resistance sets in.
Instinctively we know
 that is not right.
Each has a right to
 time of his own.
Each has a right to
 to his own privacy.
To demand full account
 of every moment
  is childish stupidity.

To search with suspicion
   pockets
     closets
       letters
        cabinets
         IS ABSURD.

Marriage demands TRUST.
Each has to be trusted enough
  so he can be what he has to be
  and become what he has to become.

*Before you find fault be sure you are
dealing with facts not figments of the
imagination.*

Care is needed lest the
IMPERSONAL ATTITUDES
in business
infect the personal
emotional response in marriage.
If man be liberated
  from stereotypes,
  he can lead a fuller life.
Why can't a man cry?
Is he less a man
  if he expresses a deep inner feeling?

Is he more a man
  if he is tough
          aggressive
          impersonal
          ambitious
          unfeeling?

*The young man who has not wept is a
savage and the old man who will not
laugh is a fool.*

— George Santayana

Often facts are blurred
   when partners carry on
   like wounded lions
      because of DISAGREEMENT.
Mature discussion needs
   calm and quiet.

Got a gripe?
Jot it down,
Seal it tight in a jar.
Once a week, set the stage
   good meal
   soft music
   candle light.
Open the jar
   and discuss the contents.

In the tranquility and calm
   of rational discussion
   "the crooked paths are made straight
   and the hills are brought low."

*We might as well give up the fiction
That we can argue any view
For what in me is pure conviction
Is simply prejudice in you.*
                    — Phyllis McGinley

friendship thrives and grows on time care and attention

"WE HAVE
  a good friendship.
Let's not
  spoil it
  by getting married."

Unfortunately,
  This statement
  is too true.

Partners ought to be
  not only lovers
  but best FRIENDS.

Every marriage
  has to maintain
  all characteristics
  of FRIENDSHIP.*

*See author's I LIKE YOU just BECAUSE

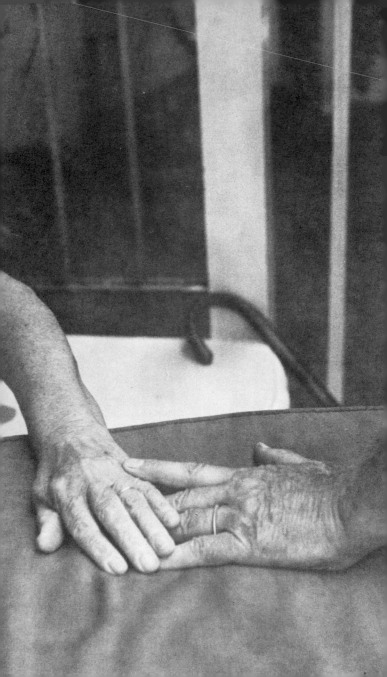

"Love means
 you never have to say
 you are sorry."
This is a stupid cliche.
It presumes that
 people in love
 are acmes of perfection.
No one is perfect.
We all belong to
 the weakened human race.
Marriage does not
 shed human nature.
Because of human limitations
 we are prone to foolish mistakes.
We all need erasers on pencils.
For human beings
 love means one must be ready
 and willing at all times to say
 I am sorry
 I am sorry for my insensitivity
 I am sorry for my preoccupation
 I am sorry for my absurdities
 I am sorry for my contradictions.
What makes it so beautiful is
 where there is true love
 there is ready forgiveness.

If you can say
  I am sorry
  and I can say
  I am sorry,
      OUR LOVE has a chance
      TO GROW.

Because neither is
  clairvoyant or transparent
  COMMUNICATION is essential.
Communication is
  more than words.

What the mouth utters
  and the ear hears
  can be belied
    by a grimace
      by dancing eyes
        by a curling lip
          by a tilt of the head.
The message sent
  is not always
  same as message received.
In all communication
  we must take into account
    mood
      timing
        context.
A childish
  stupid, juvenile
  way to handle
  any situation
  is the iceberg treatment.

*I heard every word you said. Now tell
me what you mean.*

"We ain't speaking."
To cut through
  the frigid silence
  all one can do
  is GUESS.
This is like
  Russian roulette.
Guess wrong —
  the situation
  EXPLODES.

Man is only creature
  who can communicate
  BY WORD OF MOUTH.
Nature intends
  that we do so
  especially in our
  intimate inter-personal concerns.
It is better
  to stumble through
  a halting verbal exchange
  than a witless stony silence.
Most of us hear
  only what we want to hear.
We exercise our mind
  by jumping to conclusions.
We categorize.
We grunt monosyllables.
We crowd others into a corner.

*Talking it over is an art that must be
cultivated.*

Out and out lying
   usually is not
   the big problem.

What creates a problem
   is failure to bring
   the TRUTH
   out in the open.

TRUTH is of
   the essence in marriage.

A marriage is
   not strengthened
   by telling little lies
   by hiding little things
   by masquerading
   by playing games.

Every time
   truth is hidden,
   a chance to enrich
   the marriage bond
   is lost.

Marriage is a
  difficult, demanding
  CHALLENGE.
But perhaps
  we complicate it
  too much.

Stripped to the bone,
  it is a HUMAN RELATIONSHIP
  in which each
  seeks fulfillment
      by being valued by someone
      by being aided by someone
      by being needed by someone
      by being trusted by someone
      by being oneself with someone
      by being true to someone
      by being able to share with someone.

"I Do" means facing reality.
Reality demands hard work.
Hard work is eased by communication.
Communication leads to love.
Love creates unity.
                    — Christopher Notes

Accept
Appreciate
Approve

One has to learn
 TO LISTEN
 to what partner is saying
 or trying to say but cannot.

In all communication
 it is important
 to give each other
    a sense of security
    a feeling of worth
    a healthy self-image
      an abiding self-acceptance
      a strong self-confidence.

No one is self sufficient.
A wife wants her husband
 to understand her
   to affirm her
   to assure her.

A husband wants his wife
 to understand him
   to affirm him
   to assure him.

We all have moments of
   self-doubt.
We need support.
The attitude a person
   has toward HIMSELF
   will deeply affect
   his attitude toward OTHERS.

To succeed in a
   PERSON to PERSON relationship
   one must first succeed
   AS A PERSON within himself.

The one person
   who can give you
   effective help
   and to whom
   you can give
   effective help
     is the one person
       to whom you can
       honestly and sincerely say
       of course
       I LOVE YOU.

I LOVE YOU
  not only for what you are
  but for what I am
    when I am with you.
I LOVE YOU
  not only for what you
  have made of yourself
    but what you are making
    of me.
I LOVE YOU
  for the part of me
    that you bring out.
I LOVE YOU
  for putting your hand
    into my heaped-up heart
    and passing over
      the foolish and weak things
      that you can't help seeing there.
And drawing out into the light
  all the beautiful belongings
  that no one else looked
  quite far enough to find.

I LOVE YOU
  because you are helping me to make
    of the lumber of my life
      not a tavern
      but a temple.
    Out of the works, of my every day
      not a reproach
      but a song.
I LOVE YOU
  because you have done
  more than any creed could have done
    to make me feel my goodness.
YOU HAVE DONE IT
  with your touch
    with your words
    with yourself.

123

PRAYER FOR EACH OTHER

Keep us, O Lord, from pettiness.
Let us be thoughtful in word and deed.
Help us to put away pretense
    and face each other in deep trust
    without fear or self-pity.
Let us be done with fault-finding
    and be quick to discover the best
    in every situation.
Guard us from ill temper and hasty judgment.
Encourage us to take time for all things;
    to grow calm, serene and gentle.
Help us to be swift with kind words.
Teach us never to ignore,
    never to hurt,
    never to take each other for granted.
Engrave charity and compassion on our hearts.

GRATEFUL ACKNOWLEDGEMENTS:

Artwork—Eleanor Dvorak; banners—Paula Price; jacket design—George Joseph & Associates; typists—Mary Cichowski, Virginia Flens; **Prayer for Each Other** courtesy of RESTORATION; **I Love You** courtesy of Mrs. Henry Powell; photography assistance—Joseph Reiter.

PHOTO CREDITS:

Courtesy of GTE Sylvania Incorporated 8; Ed Carlin 115; Patti Carroll 27, 72, 90, 91, 103, 106; Rohn Engh 118, 125; Bonnie Grota & Joseph Reiter 108; G & J Kaminski 20, 35; Aligimantas Kezys S.J. Courtesy of Loyola University Press 33, 39, 40, 55, 64, 69, 79, 80, 110, 116; Jean-Claude Le Juene 13, 15, 17, 28, 37, 45, 48, 50, 53, 62, 66, 76, 87, 96, 98; "Iggy" by Joe Reiter Jr. 43, 94; Robert Wagner 60, 70, 89;.

Please send _____

of course

I LOVE YOU $3.50
Albert J. Nimeth O.F.M.

From your bookstore, or   FRANCISCAN HERALD PRESS
1434 WEST 51st STREET • CHICAGO, 6060

Name_____

Address_____

City_____

State_____ Zip____

Please add .25c for handling.

Please send _____

I LIKE YOU JUST BECAUSE $3.50

by Albert J. Nimeth O.F.M.

From your bookstore, or   FRANCISCAN HERALD PRESS
1434 WEST 51st STREET • CHICAGO, 60609

Name_____

Address_____

City_____

State_____ Zip_____

Please add .25c for handling.